W9-BYS-525

DISCARDED

WEATHER WORDS

AND WHAT THEY MEAN

BY GAIL GIBBONS

HOLIDAY HOUSE
NEW YORK

For John Briggs

Special thanks to the National Weather Service in Burlington, Vermont, and to Chris Vaccaro of the National Oceanic and Atmospheric Administration

Copyright © 1990, 2019 by Gail Gibbons
All Rights Reserved
HOLIDAY HOUSE is registered in the U.S. Patent and Trademark Office.
Printed & Bound in July 2018
at Tien Wah Press, Johor Bahru, Johor, Malaysia.
Second Edition
www.holidayhouse.com
1 3 5 7 9 10 8 6 4 2

The Library of Congress has catalogued the prior edition as follows:
Gibbons, Gail.
Weather words and what they mean / by Gail Gibbons.
p. cm.
Summary: Introduces basic weather terms and concepts.
ISBN 0-8234-0805-1
1. Weather—Terminology—Juvenile literature.
2. Meteorology—Terminology—Juvenile literature.
[1. Weather—Terminology.
2. Meteorology—Terminology.]
I. Title. QC981.3.G53 1990
551.6'014—dc20 89-39515 CIP AC
ISBN 0-8234-0805-1
ISBN 0-8234-0952-X (pbk.)
New and Updated Edition

ISBN 978-0-8234-4171-6 (hardcover)
ISBN 978-0-8234-4190-7 (paperback)

The weather changes from day to day. Weather words explain what the weather is like outside.

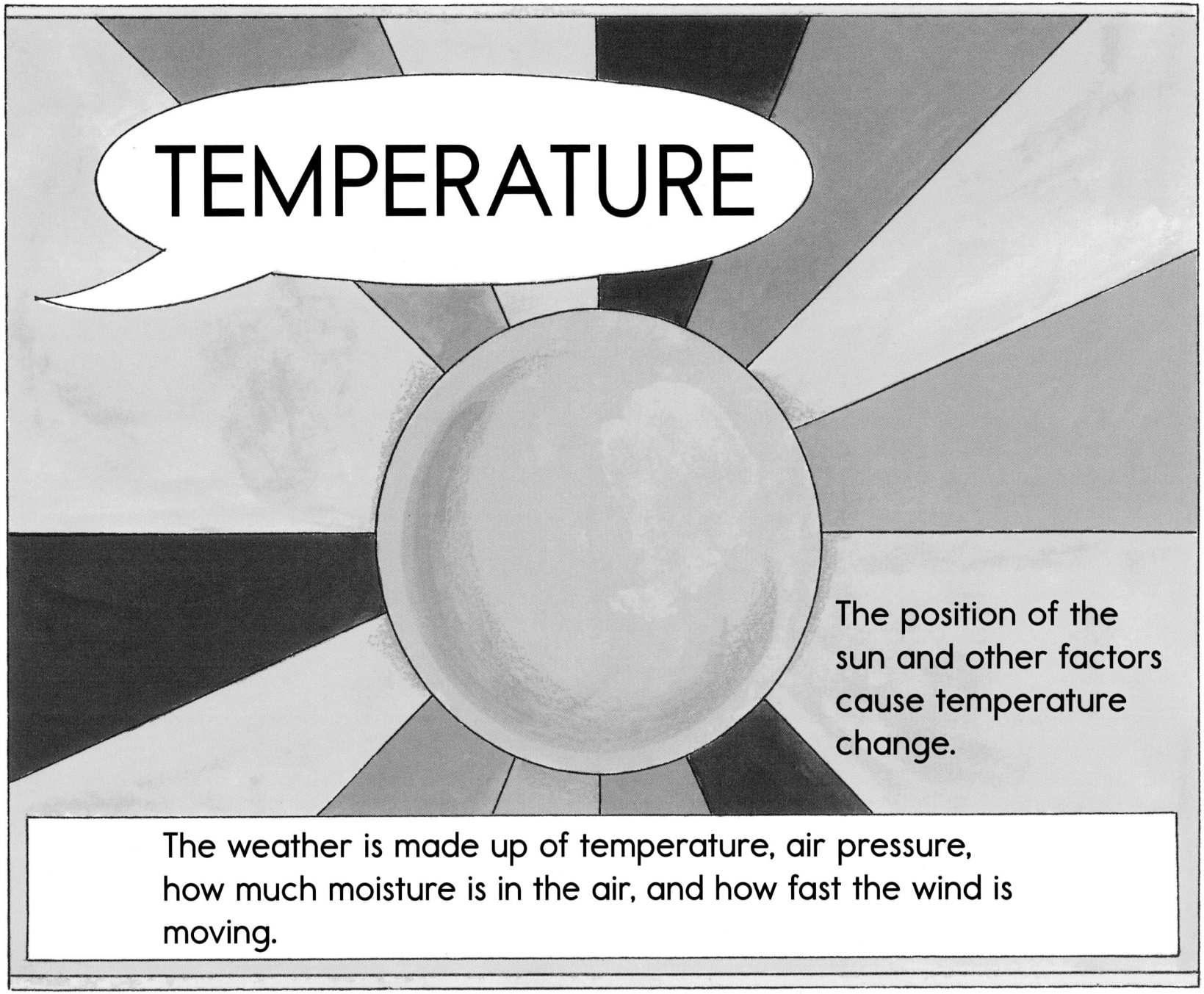
TEMPERATURE
The position of the sun and other factors cause temperature change.
The weather is made up of temperature, air pressure, how much moisture is in the air, and how fast the wind is moving.

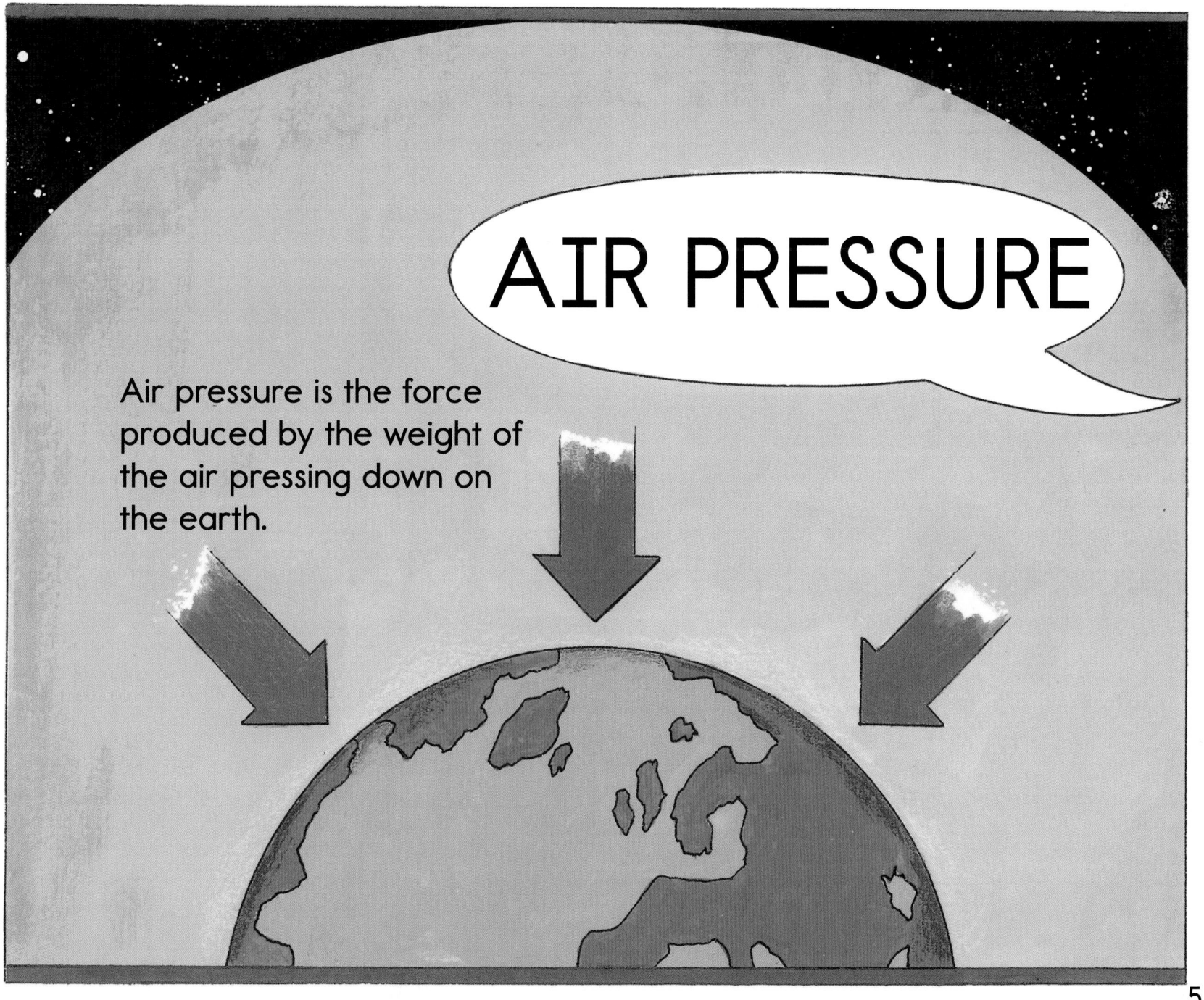
AIR PRESSURE
Air pressure is the force produced by the weight of the air pressing down on the earth.

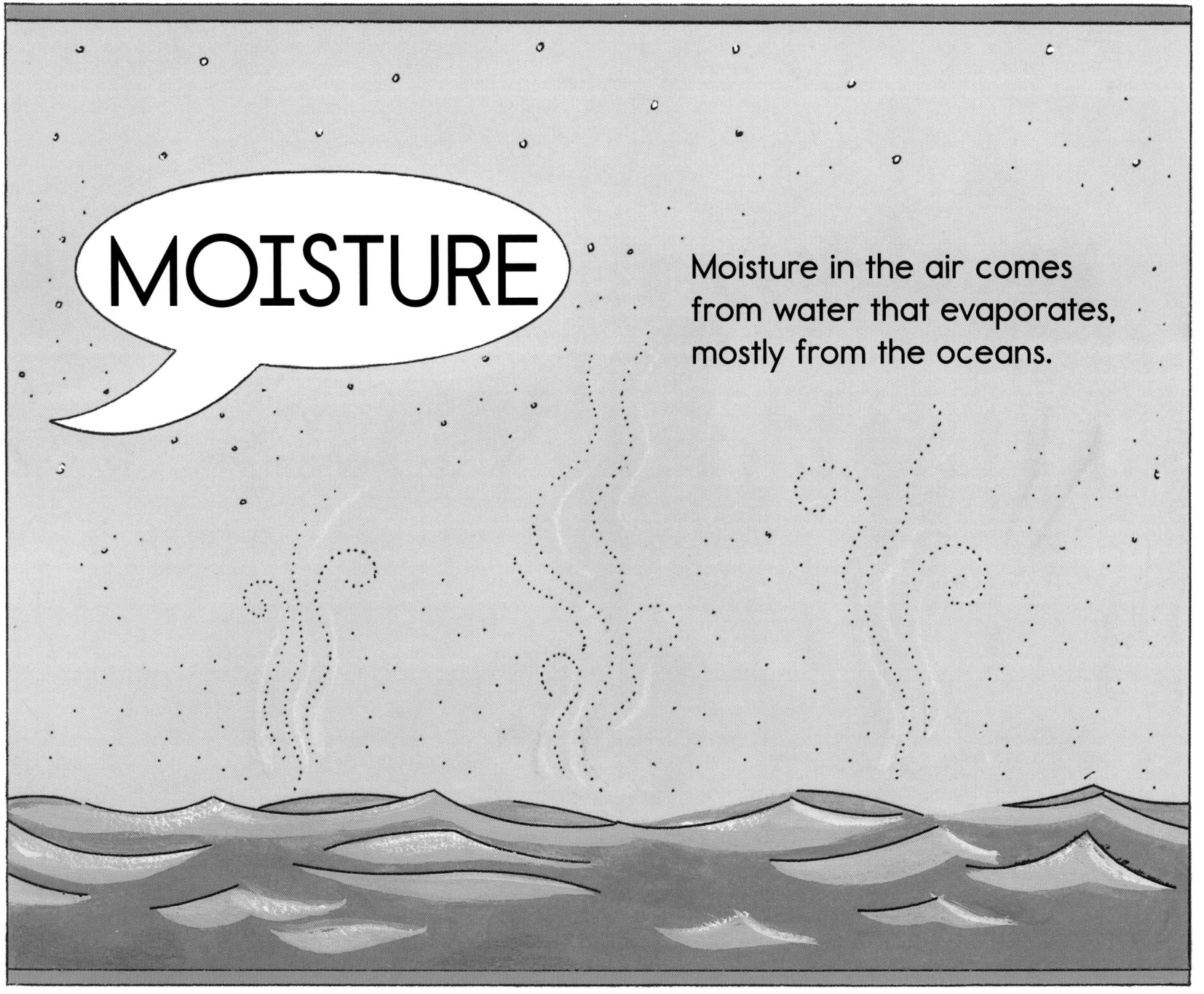
MOISTURE
Moisture in the air comes from water that evaporates, mostly from the oceans.

Wind is air in motion.

TEMPERATURE

HOT
The temperature also changes with the seasons. In the summer, the sun is high in the sky. The days are warm and longer.
WARM
COLD
In the winter, the sun is low in the sky. The days are cold and shorter.

AIR PRESSURE

High pressure is when air particles are close together. The air is usually cool and dry. High pressure often brings fair weather.

HIGH PRESSURE

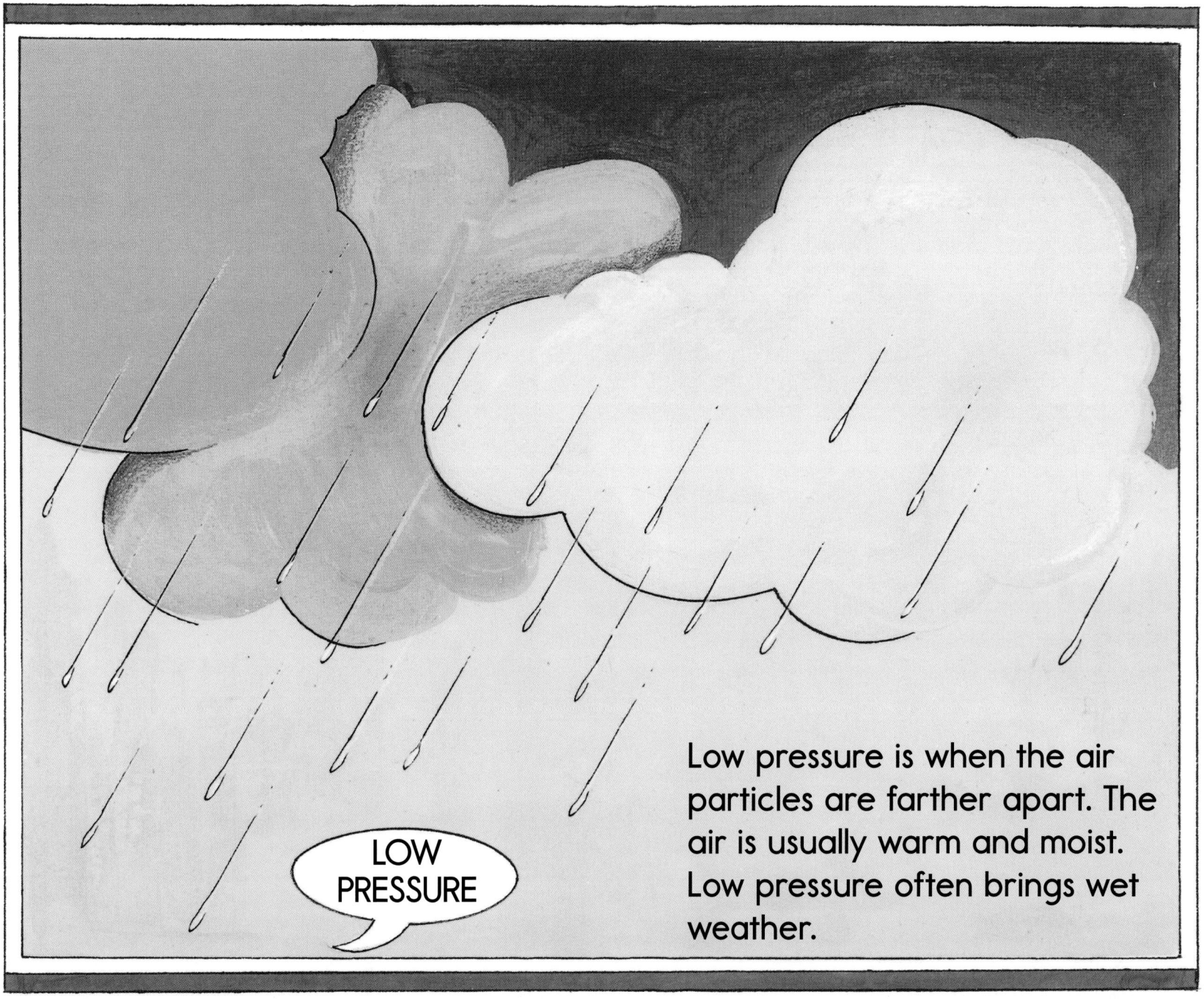

Low pressure is when the air particles are farther apart. The air is usually warm and moist. Low pressure often brings wet weather.

MOISTURE

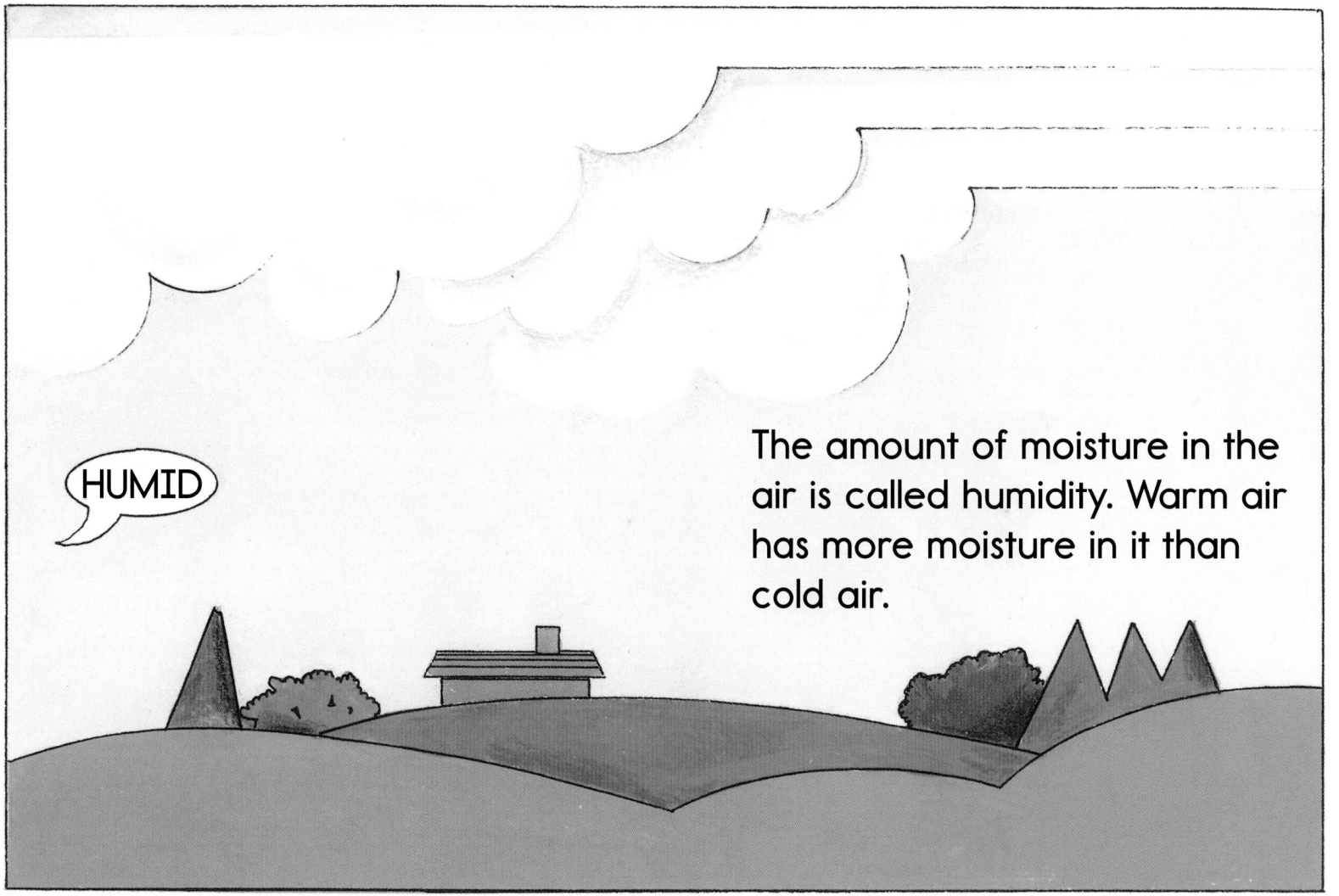

The amount of moisture in the air is called humidity. Warm air has more moisture in it than cold air.

At night when the air cools down, it can't hold as much moisture. The moisture that forms on the ground is called dew.
DEW
If the temperature goes below freezing, the dew freezes. Then it is called frost.
FROST

Moisture makes clouds, too. When water evaporates from rivers, lakes, and oceans, it is called vapor. It moves up with the warm air and forms little drops of water or ice crystals. A cloud is formed.

Clouds come in all shapes and sizes. There are three main kinds of clouds.

There are other kinds of clouds with long names. They are combinations of cumulus, cirrus, and stratus clouds.

Altostratus clouds
often bring rain or snow.

PARTLY
CLOUDY
Altocumulus clouds
can bring showers
or snow flurries.
Sometimes the sun
shines through them.

CLOUDY
Stratocumulus clouds
usually are winter clouds.

Cumulonimbus clouds
are thunderstorm
clouds.

A cloud close to the earth's surface is called fog.
FOG

Rain forms inside rain clouds. The water vapor that evaporates from below forms tiny water drops.
The tiny drops join together and become bigger drops.
When they are heavy enough, they fall.
RAIN

Rain comes down in different ways.

Sometimes there are floods when heavy rain falls or when it rains for a long time.
FLOODS

THUNDERSTORM
Thunderstorms can be powerful and noisy! Lots of tiny drops of water whip around inside the cloud at very high speeds.
When they rub and bump against each other, they make electricity.

When enough electricity builds up, it bursts through the cloud and flashes. This is called lightning. Lightning is very hot. It heats the air around it. The hot air expands and . . . BOOM! It makes a loud noise called thunder.

Everyone loves looking at a rainbow! This may happen while it is raining, or just after the rain stops. When sunbeams shine through drops of rain, the light breaks up into seven colors. A rainbow appears.

Sometimes in the winter it snows. Snow crystals form when moisture freezes inside the clouds.
When the snow crystals join together, they become snowflakes.
When they are heavy enough, they fall.
SNOW

Snow falls to the earth in different ways.

Sometimes it hails. Inside the cloud ice crystals are tossed up and down. Water vapor freezes onto the ice crystals in layers. When they become heavy enough, they fall as hailstones. Hailstones can be as small as a pea or as big as a baseball.

WIND

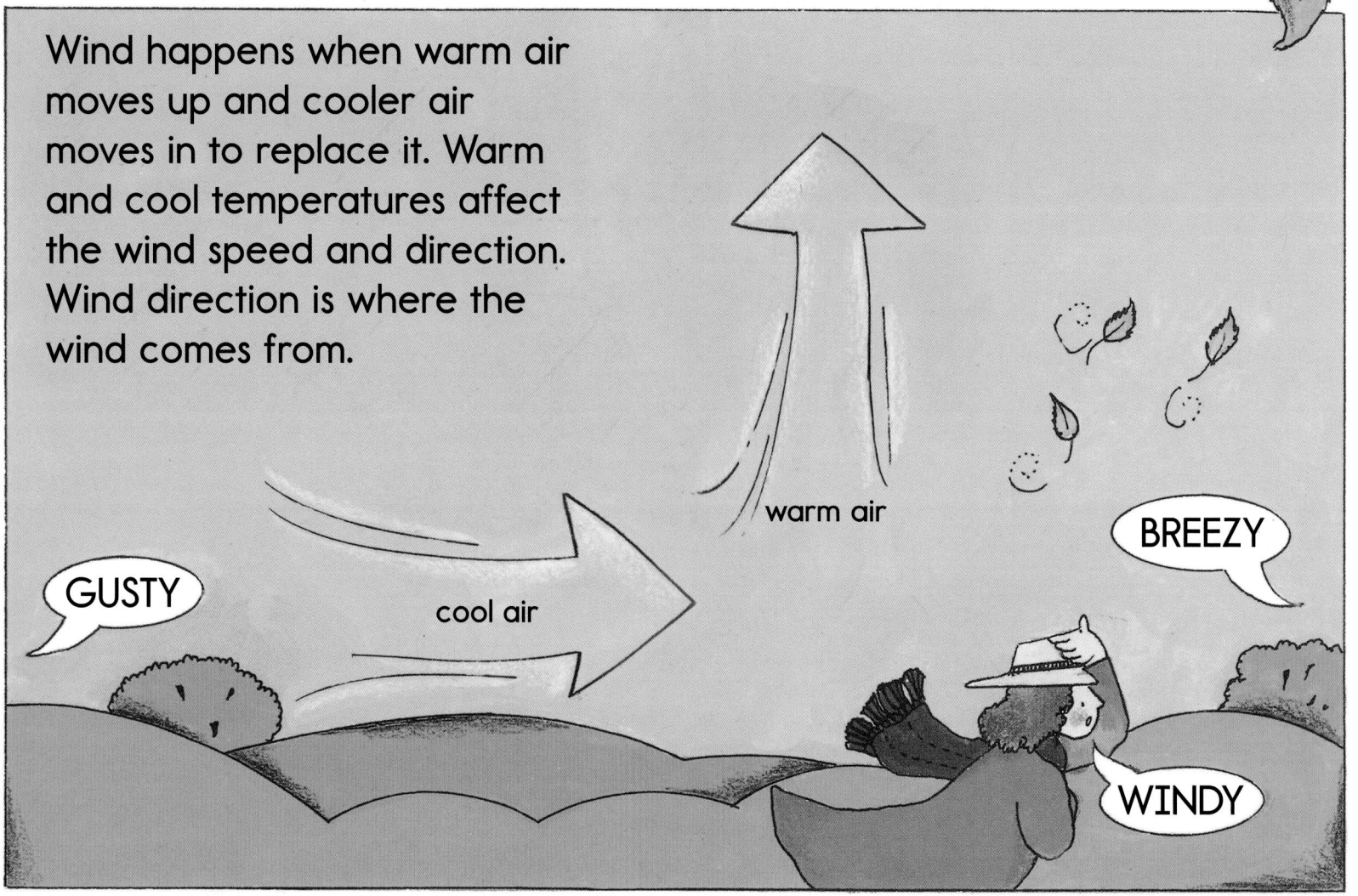

Wind happens when warm air moves up and cooler air moves in to replace it. Warm and cool temperatures affect the wind speed and direction. Wind direction is where the wind comes from.

When wind blows with more and more force, a windstorm develops. There are many kinds of windstorms. Often, they cause damage.

The many combinations of temperature, air pressure, moisture, and wind create different kinds of weather conditions. A big area of weather that is the same is called an air mass. The boundary between two air masses is called a front. This boundary is where the weather changes.

The weather is hardly ever the same from day to day.
That's why it is so interesting.

31333049386434

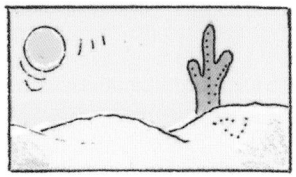

The driest non-polar place in the world is the Atacama Desert in Chile.

A number of years ago in France, a tornado crossed a pond and sucked up everything. At the place where the tornado stopped, the people had a surprise rainfall of fish and frogs!

There is enough electricity in one flash of lightning to light a small town for one day.

It rains more days each year on Kauai, Hawaii, than in any other place in the world. There it rains about 350 days a year.

The highest wind speed ever recorded was 253 miles per hour in 1996 on Australia's Barrow Island.

Sound travels at 1,125 feet per second. If you are one mile from lightning, it will take about five seconds for the sound of thunder to reach you.

The coldest recorded temperature was in Antarctica. It was –128° Fahrenheit (–89.2° Centigrade).

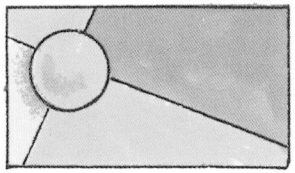

The hottest recorded temperature was in Death Valley, California. It was 134° Fahrenheit (56.7° Centigrade). Most scientists think the earth is getting warmer and that this is changing weather patterns.

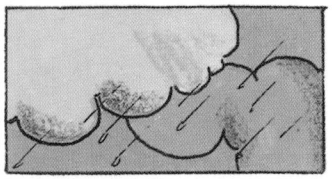

REMEMBER . . .

When you hear a weather forecast that gives storm warnings, pay attention. Be careful.